LIGHTNING BOLT BOOKS™

Experiment with Parts of a Plant

Nadia Higgins

Lerner Publications
Minneapolis

Content Consultant: Dr. Norm Lownds, Curator, Michigan 4-H Children's Gardens

Lerner Publications Company
A division of Lerner Publishing Group, Inc.
241 First Avenue North
Minneapolis, MN 55401 USA

For reading levels and more information, look up this title at www.lernerbooks.com.

Library of Congress Cataloging-in-Publication Data

Higgins, Nadia.
     Experiment with parts of a plant / by Nadia Higgins.
          pages   cm. — (Lightning bolt books™—Plant experiments)
     Includes index.
     ISBN 978-1-4677-5733-1 (lib. bdg. : alk. paper)
     ISBN 978-1-4677-6074-4 (pbk.)
     ISBN 978-1-4677-6244-1 (EB pdf)
     1. Plants—Juvenile literature. 2. Plants—Experiments—Juvenile literature. I. Title. II. Series:
     Lightning bolt books. Plant experiments.
     QK49.H538 2015
     580—dc23   2014027533

Manufactured in the United States of America
1 – BP – 12/31/14

Table of Contents

How Much Water Do Roots Take In?

Can you name some of the parts of this plant?

Roots, stems, leaves, flowers, fruits, and seeds— it's easy to remember a plant's six parts. They sound just like a poem!

leaves

fruit

stem

flower

root

seeds

A plant's parts work together to keep it alive.

Each plant part has several jobs. The main job of roots, stems, and leaves is to help a plant grow. Flowers, fruits, and seeds help a plant produce new plants.

Mosses don't have flowers or seeds.

Not all plants have every part. Stems, leaves, flowers, fruits, and seeds can all come and go during the life of a plant. All plants have roots, though.

Most roots take in water from the soil. The water holds minerals the plant needs to stay healthy. Let's look at how much water roots take in.

What You Need:

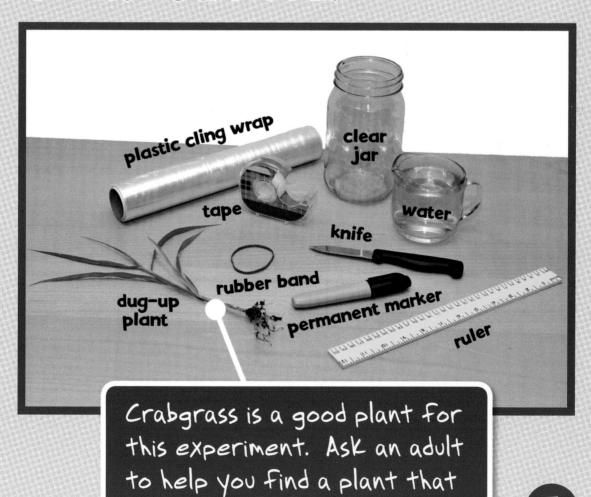

plastic cling wrap

clear jar

tape

water

knife

dug-up plant

rubber band

permanent marker

ruler

Crabgrass is a good plant for this experiment. Ask an adult to help you find a plant that is safe to dig up.

Steps:

1. Fill the jar with water almost to the top.

2. Cover the jar tightly with the plastic cling wrap. Use the rubber band to hold the plastic wrap in place.

Mark the water level on the jar with the marker.

3. Have an adult use the knife to cut a slit across the middle of the plastic cling wrap.

4. Gently push the plant's stem through the slit in the plastic wrap. Tape around the plant's stem to seal up the slit. Then put the jar in a sunny spot.

The plastic wrap will keep the water from evaporating.

5. After three days, take the plant out of the jar. Measure how far the water level has fallen in the jar.

Many factors play a role in how much water the roots took up. A plant's health or when it was last watered can make a difference.

Think It Through

Roots can take in a lot of water. Were you surprised by how much water the roots took up? Try this experiment with a different plant. First, predict how much water the new plant's roots will take up. Then see if your prediction was correct!

Some roots, such as carrots, have an extra job. They store food for the plant.

What Do Plant Stems Do?

A plant's stem has an important job. The stem holds up the plant. This lets the leaves reach sunlight so they can make food.

A vine has a very long stem. The vine holds itself up by climbing things around it.

Tree trunks are stems that bring a tree's leaves closer to the sun.

A stem is also a pathway. Water from the roots goes up the stem. Food from the leaves goes down.

We can experiment to prove that water travels up through the stem. Let's find out what happens when you put carnation stems in colored water.

What You Need:

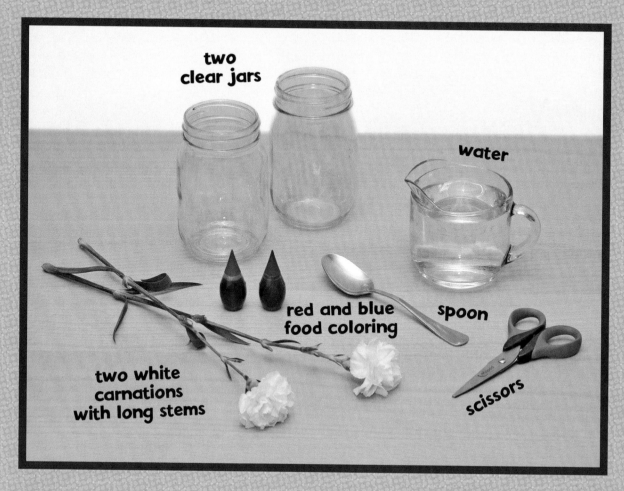

two clear jars

water

red and blue food coloring

spoon

two white carnations with long stems

scissors

Steps:

1. Fill the jars a little more than halfway with water.

2. Add 30 drops of red food coloring to one jar. Then add 30 drops of blue food coloring to the other. Stir the water in each jar well.

The more food coloring you add, the more obvious the experiment's results will be!

Now let's see what happens when you put the flowers in the water!

3. Trim the bottom of the stems with scissors.

4. Put one stem in each jar.

Make sure each stem is long enough to reach the bottom of its jar.

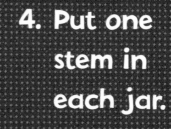

Wait a few hours. What happened?

The water turned your flowers red and blue!

Think It Through

The colored water moved up the stems. Try this experiment again with different colors.

Do Leaves Give Off More Water in Hot Weather?

Leaves give off water through a process called transpiration. Water evaporates through tiny holes in the leaf called stomates.

Green leaves use water, along with sunlight and air, to make sugar through photosynthesis.

Let's watch stomates at work!

What You Need:

two leafy potted plants

two clear plastic bags

two twist ties

water

Geraniums work well for this experiment.

Steps:

1. Water both plants well. Then cover each plant with a bag.

2. Use the twist ties to close the bags around each plant and its pot.

A sunny windowsill is the perfect place for one of your plants.

3. Put one plant in a warm, sunny spot. Put the second plant in a cool spot that still gets some light.

4. Leave your plants for one full day. Then carefully remove the plastic bags.

Compare the two bags. What do you see?

The plant in the warm, sunny spot gave off much more water.

Think It Through

The bag in the sunny spot had more water droplets on it than the bag in the cool spot. Plants give off more water in the heat. That helps cool them down, just as sweat cools people down.

How Do Seeds Move?

A flower's job is to make seeds. One way or another, those seeds need to be spread away from the plant. Otherwise, young plants will crowd the parent plant like weeds.

Seeds can grow inside tasty fruit, such as apples. The sweet fruit lures hungry people and animals. They pick up the fruit and carry it away.

Seeds can move in many different ways. Some seeds move by wind. Others move by water. Some even travel using people or animals. Let's look at how different seeds move!

Some wind-blown seeds have parts to catch the breeze.

What You Need:

Ask an adult to help you gather four different types of seeds. Maple tree seeds, peapods, acorns, and pinecones work well.

fan

masking tape

four different seeds

Steps:

1. Study each seed closely. Then make a prediction about how far each seed will move.

2. Set up your fan to blow across the room. Put a piece of tape on the ground a few inches in front of the fan.

The tape marks the spot where you will drop the seeds.

3. Turn the fan on high. Drop one of your seeds in front of the fan.

4. Repeat with the other three seeds. Make sure to drop all of your seeds from the same height.

Think It Through

Did one seed go farther than the others? That seed is probably transported by wind. Were your predictions correct about how far each seed would go?

A coconut is one of the world's largest seeds. It floats away on ocean waves.

Classify Like a Scientist

Plant parts help scientists classify plants, or put them into categories. The next time you're in a garden, invent your own system for sorting plants. Use these tips as a guide:

1. Start big. What do most of the plants have in common?

2. Break it down. Keep looking for differences and similarities. Maybe some leaves are all one shade of green, while others are striped or spotted.

3. Be specific. Instead of classifying grasses as tall, classify them as "higher than my knees."

Fun Facts

- A broom plant spreads its seeds by itself. Its seedpods heat up in the sun. Then—pop! They burst open, and seeds go flying.

- Sticky burdock seeds gave one inventor the idea for Velcro.

- Broccoli is really a flower.

- One-tenth of the water in Earth's atmosphere comes from plants.

- The first flowers appeared on Earth approximately 130 million years ago.

Glossary

evaporate: to turn from a liquid to a gas

mineral: a substance that living things need to stay healthy

predict: to make a good guess about what might happen in the future

stomate: a small opening on the underside of a leaf

transpiration: the way water moves through a plant and goes out the leaves into the air

Further Reading

Duke, Shirley. *Step-by-Step Experiments with Plants.* Mankato, MN: Child's World, 2012.

The Great Plant Escape
http://urbanext.illinois.edu/gpe/index.cfm

Parts of a Plant
http://kidsgrowingstrong.org/PlantParts

Salas, Laura Purdie. *A Leaf Can Be . . .* Minneapolis: Millbrook Press, 2012.

Taylor, Barbara. *Inside Plants.* New York: Marshall Cavendish Benchmark, 2010.

US Botanic Children's Garden: Interview with a Gardener
http://kids.usa.gov/watch-videos/videos/gardener/index.shtml

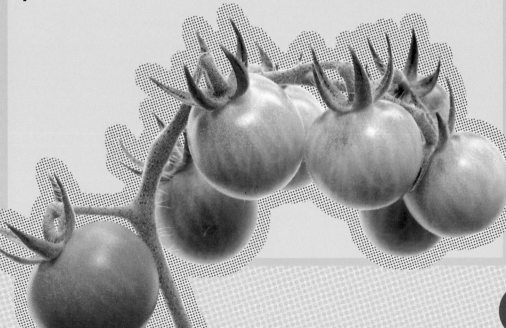

Index

Photo Acknowledgments

The images in this book are used with the permission of: © Rick Orndorf, pp. 2, 7, 8, 9, 10, 14, 15, 16, 17, 19, 20, 21, 24, 25, 26; © Jaimie Duplass/Shutterstock Images, p. 4; © BlueRingMedia/Shutterstock Images, p. 5 (plant); © Yayasya/Thinkstock, p. 5 (tomato); © Ryan McVay/Thinkstock, p. 6; © Jupiterimages/Thinkstock, pp. 11, 13; © Fuse/Thinkstock, pp. 12, 28; © sssss1gmel/Thinkstock, p. 18; © Ann-Chantal/Thinkstock, p. 22; © Foxline/Thinkstock, p. 23; © mangostock/Shutterstock Images, p. 27; © varela/Thinkstock, p. 30; © Smithore/Thinkstock, p. 31.

Front cover: © iStockphoto.com/varela.

Main body text set in Johann Light 30/36.